I LOVE YOU!

The BIG Valentine's Day

Coloring BOOK for

Toddlers & Preschool

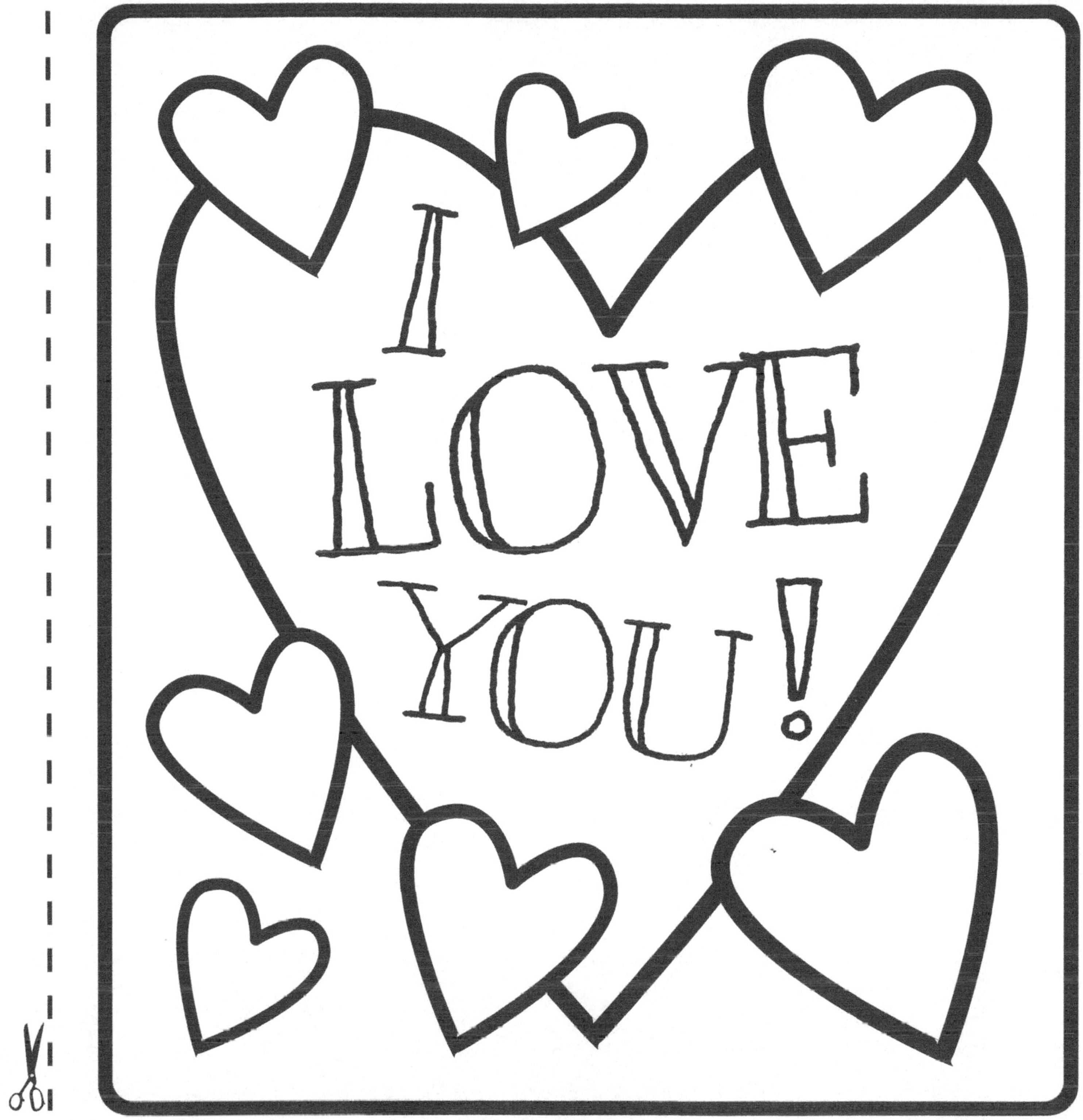
I
LOVE
YOU!

Beeeee MY VALENTINE

L IS FOR

LOVE

LOVE

LOVE

LOVE

LOVE

LOVE

LOVE

B IS FOR

BALLOONS

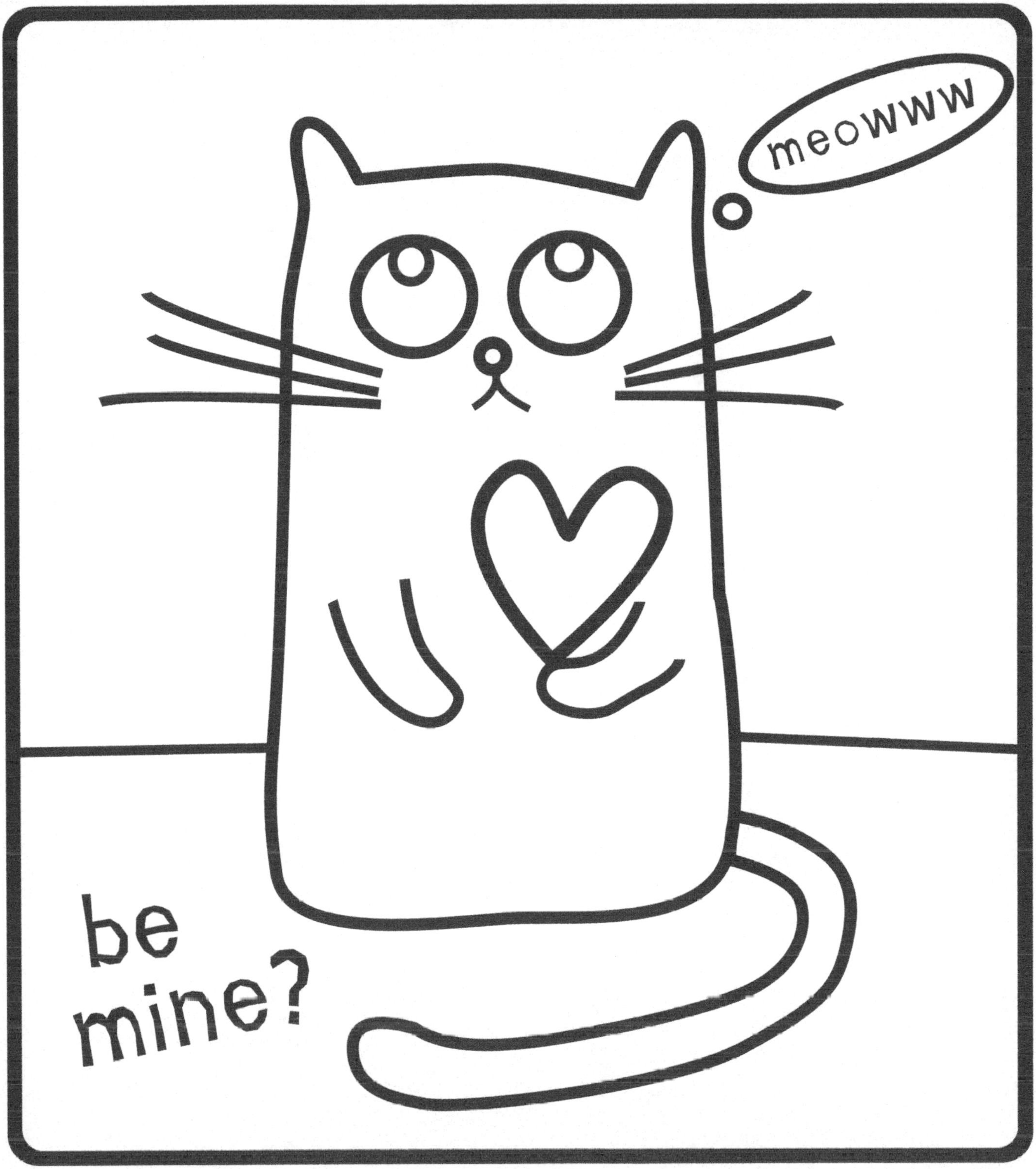
meowww
be mine?

H IS FOR HEARTS !!!

Happy

Valentine's

daY!!!

R IS FOR roses

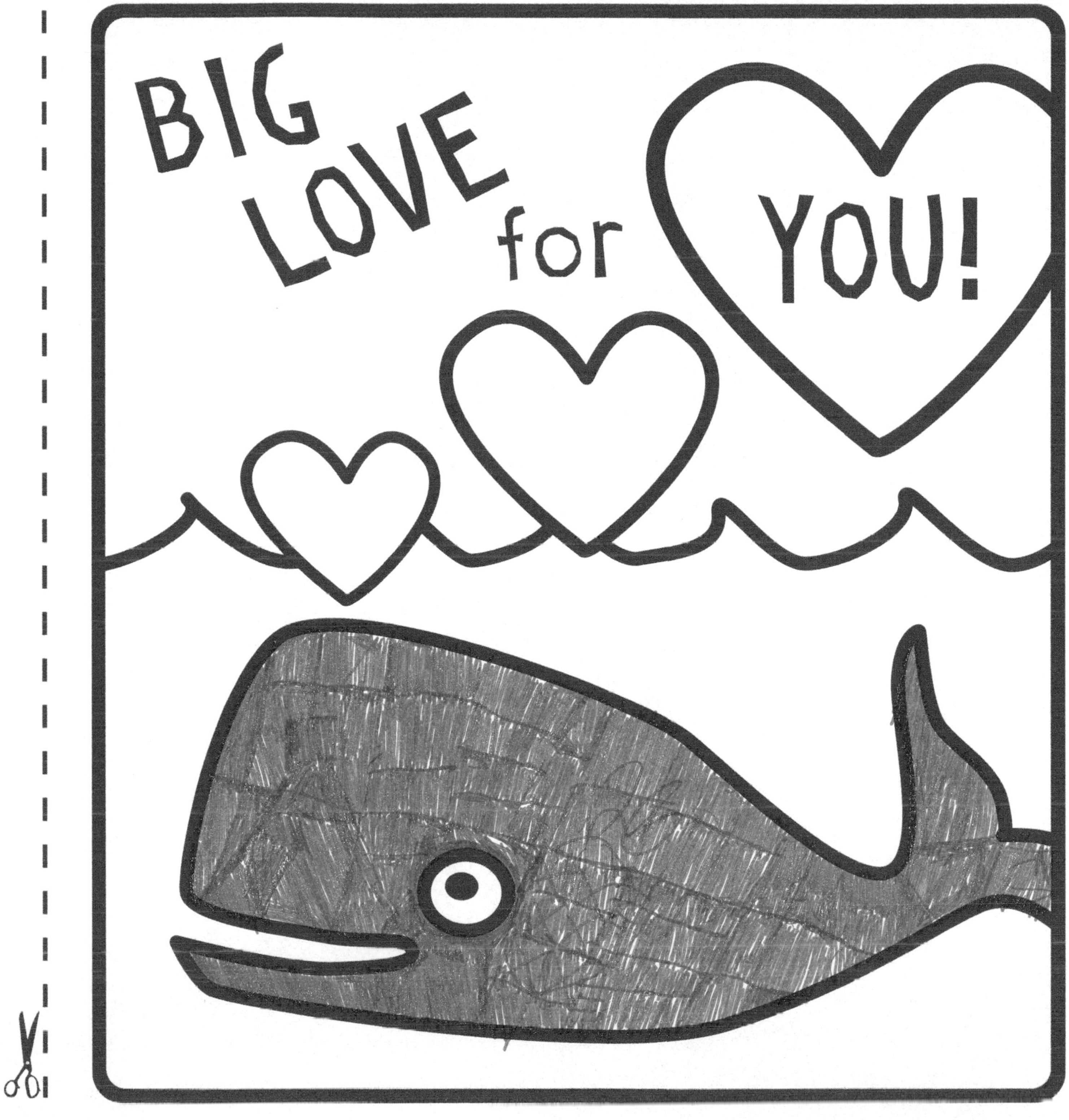
BIG LOVE for
YOU!

F IS FOR

FLOWERS

be

my

Valentine?

Together

Forever !

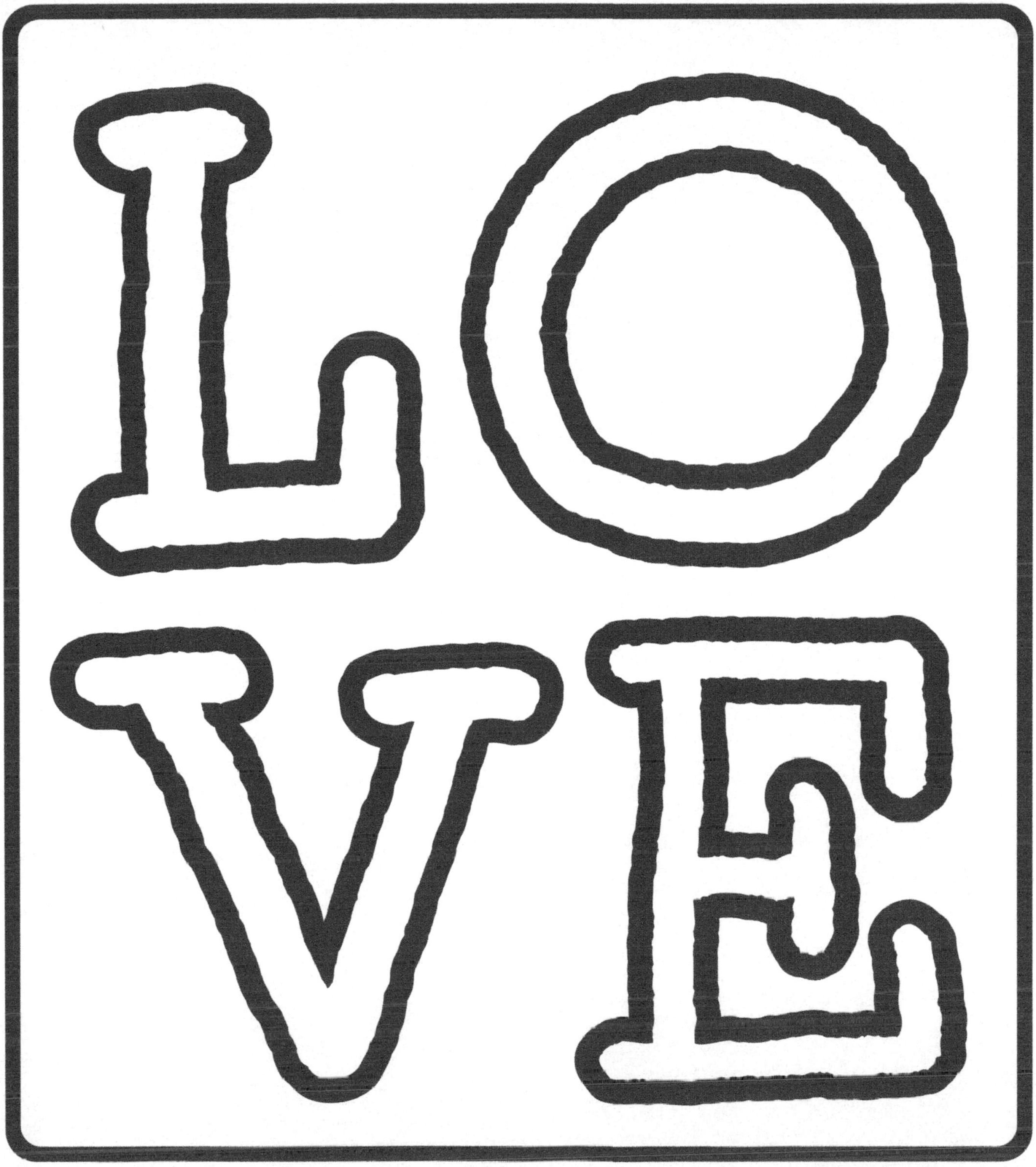
LOVE

Happy V-day!

U IS FOR

UNICORN

LOVE

YOU!

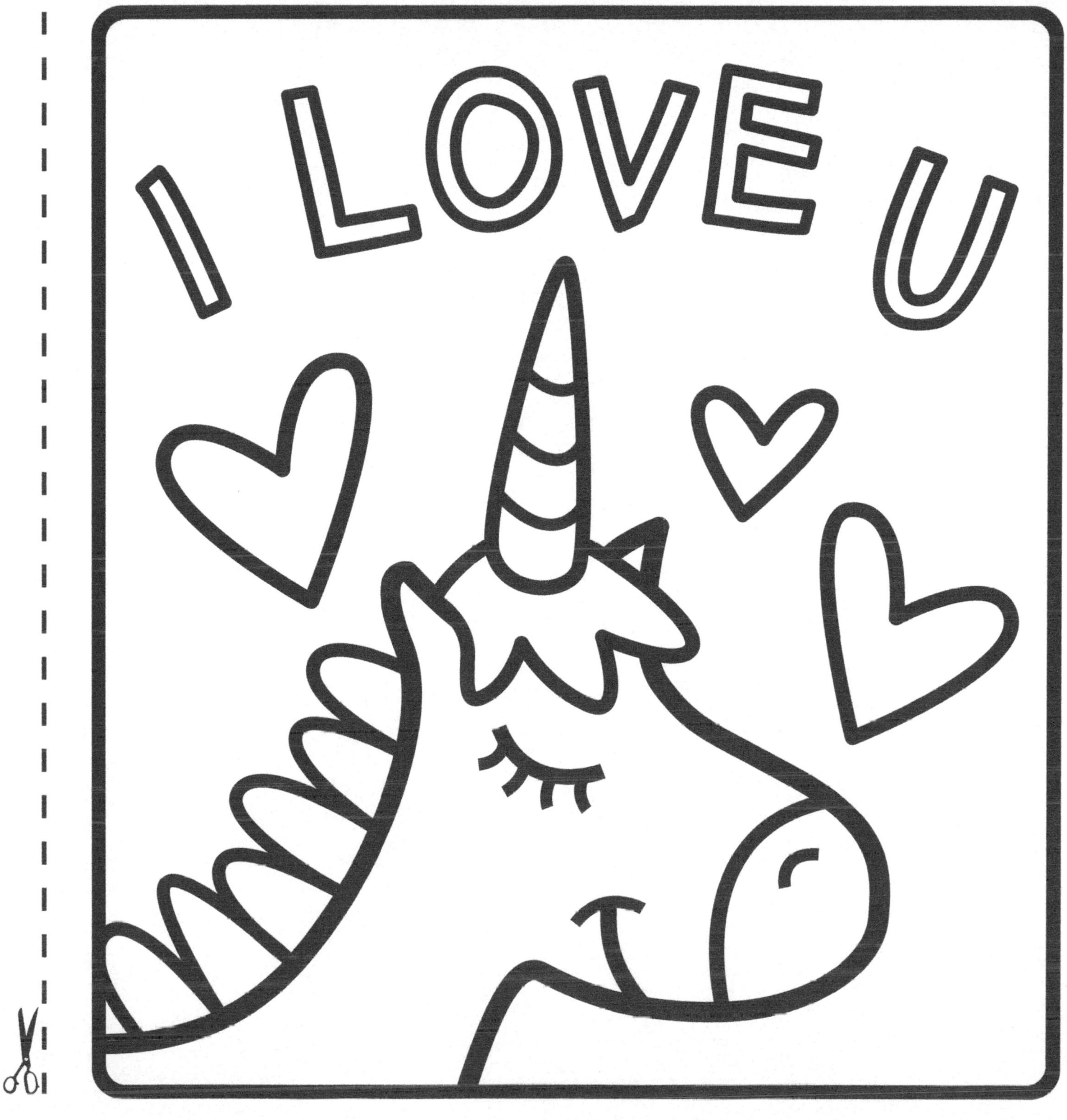
I LOVE U

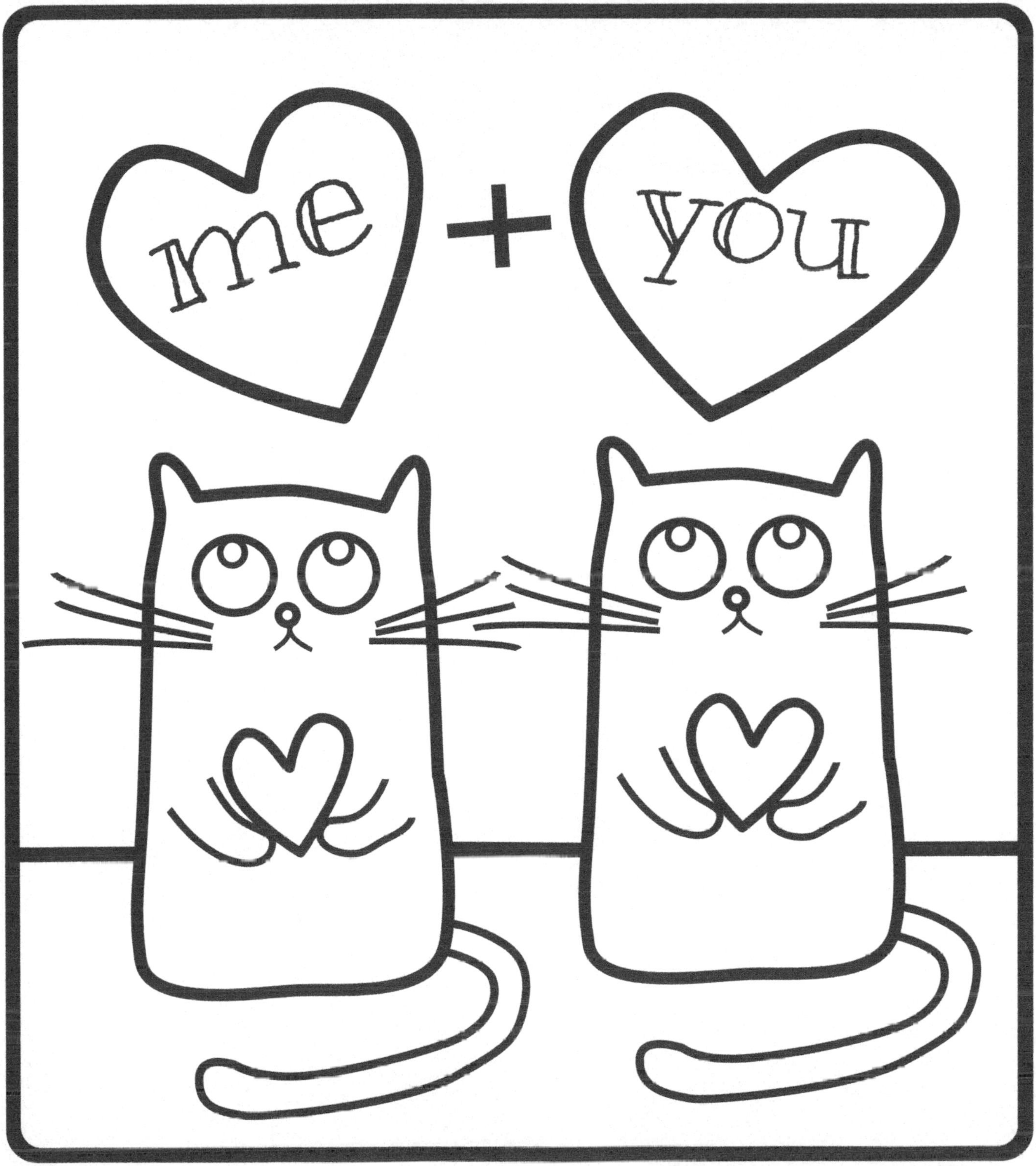
me
+
you

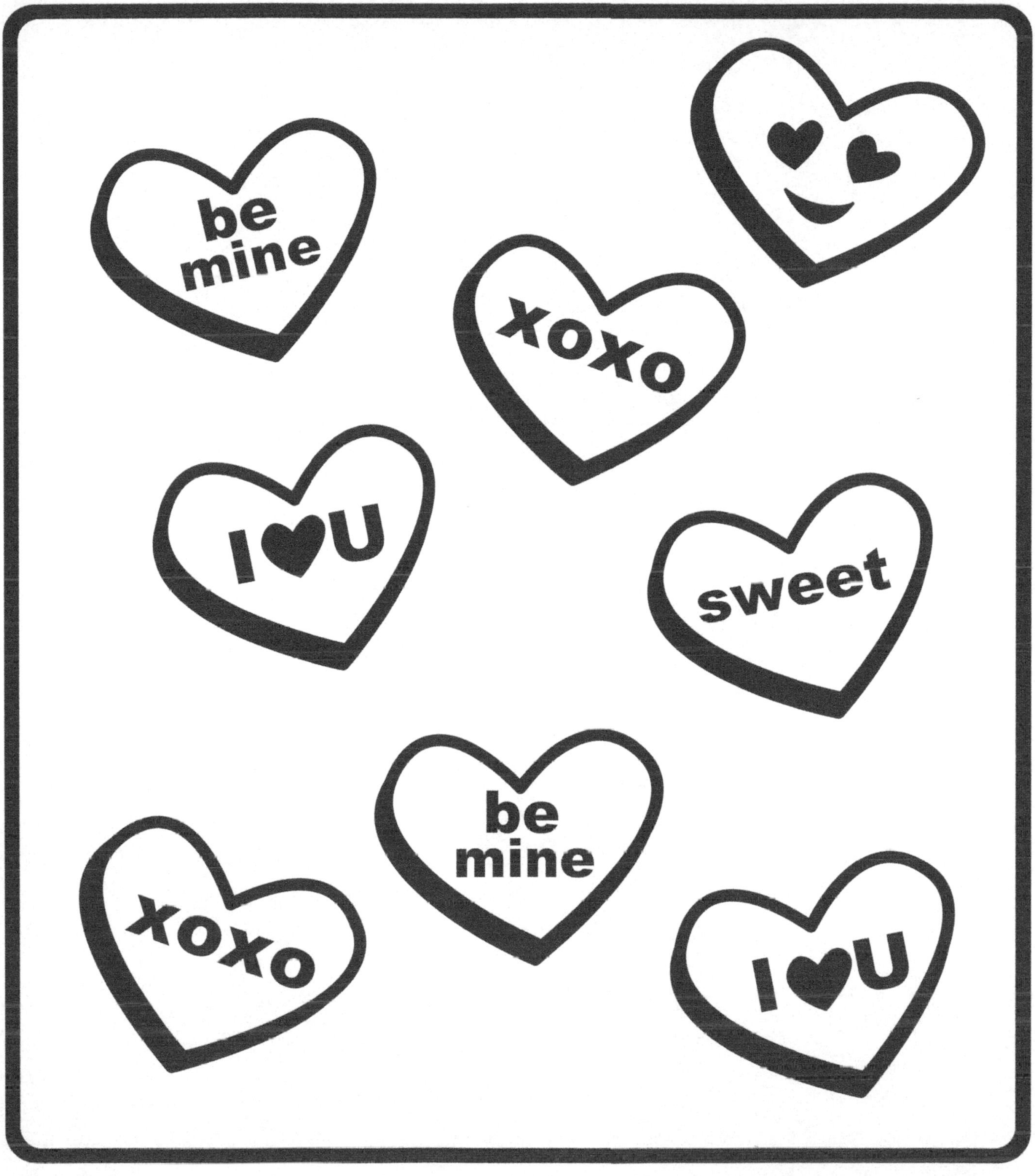
be mine
xoxo
I ♥ U
sweet
be mine
xoxo
I ♥ U

I LOVE YOU!

Happy Valentine's Day !!!

Happy Valentine's Day

i love you

u2

Made in the USA
Coppell, TX
04 February 2020